God Loves Everyone

by Jim Lo

Illustrated by Carolyn Ewing Bowser

To my family,
Roxene, Andre, and Matthew

Hi, My name is Andy Matthews.
I like going to church.
I like to hear my pastor preach
about God.

Today, my pastor said that
God loves everyone.

God loves the Herero people,
who live in Namibia, Africa.
The women there like to wear
fancy hats and long, colorful dresses.

God loves the people
who live in Ghana.
Jotham Moyo lives in a house
made from mud and grass.

Many animals live around
Jotham's home.
God also loves Jotham's mother,
who carries her baby on her back.
God loves Jotham's sister,
who carries firewood on her head.

God loves the people
who live in Nepal.
The women there
carry groceries home
in long baskets.

God loves the people
who live in India.
Raja likes to sit on a rock
and read a book.

God loves the people
who live in China.
Lo Gen Jo lives on a boat.
The boat is called a junk.

God loves the people
who live in Mexico.
This lady is hoping to sell her pottery.

God loves the Eskimos
who live in Alaska and Canada.
Some Eskimos ride on sleds
pulled by dogs.

Some Eskimos use a long harpoon
to hunt for whales.

God loves the people of Peru.
Little Marie lives in Peru.
She takes care of
her brother and sister.

God loves Marie's father.
He helps carry bananas
from the banana farm to the town.

God loves everyone.
Whether the person has red, black,
white, or yellow skin,
GOD LOVES THEM.

You may have large blue eyes
or small brown eyes
or medium green eyes.
You may have straight blond hair
or tight black hair
or short light brown hair
or curly red hair—
or no hair at all.
GOD LOVES YOU.

We are all different.
God made us that way.
AND GOD LOVES US ALL.

God so loved the world that He gave
His one and only Son, that whoever
believes in Him shall not perish but
have eternal life.

John 3:16